Living in the Grace of God

Rob Rufus

All who rely on observing the law are under a
curse . . .   (Gal. 3:10a)

When we live in the grace of God we experience a
creative flow, a joy, a spontaneity, and an
enthusiasm for life; and – we stop trying to
live up to some standard that we can never reach,
free from the feeling that God is angry with us.

Authentic

LONDON ● ATLANTA ● HYDERABAD

13 12 11 10 09 08 07   7 6 5 4 3 2 1

First published 1997 by Rob Rufus
This edition published 2007 by Authentic Media
9 Holdom Avenue, Bletchley, Milton Keynes, MK1 1QR, UK
285 Lynnwood Avenue, Tyrone, GA 30290, USA
OM Authentic Media, Medchal Road, Jeedimetla Village,
Secunderabad 500 055, A.P., India
www.authenticmedia.co.uk

Authentic Media is a division of Send the Light Ltd., a company
limited by guarantee (registered charity no. 270162)

British Library Cataloguing in Publication Data
A catalogue record for this book is available from the British Library

ISBN 978-1-86024-605-0

Rob Rufus and his wife Glenda currently lead a church based in Hong
Kong. www.citychurchinternational.com

Cover Design by fourninezero design.
Print Management by Adare Carwin
Printed in Great Britain by J.H. Haynes & Co., Sparkford

Contents

To my best friend Glenda
who always helped me to tie my dhoti

Acknowledgements

To the people who have poured grace into my life.

To the wife of my youth, Glenda – you keep on amazing me by your kindness, respect and love toward me – a depth that I do not deserve. To my dear Dad and Mom who I will always be grateful for. To Karl and Pauline Cronje, Dudley and Ann Daniel, Chris and Meryl Weinand, Fini and Isi de Gersigny, Gerald and Anona Coates, Terry and Wendy Virgo, Rodney and Adonica Howard-Browne.

To all the team of NCMI. To the people of Victory Faith Centre who so patiently endured my early developmental years as a pastor – I love you all! To the elders, deacons and people of Coastlands International Christian Centre – you are some of the most gracious people I have ever had the privilege of knowing. Your endless love and support are more precious to me than words can tell. You are a grace-filled people and your zeal for God is what inspired me to write this book.

To the awesome people of City Church International, Hong Kong – we are living the adventure of vision fulfilment together! Thank you for giving me wings to fly the dream. Your courage and kindness are a catalyst of grace that conquers all opposition and passionately pursues the prize of all prizes – his glorious presence.

I am grateful to a number of people who have assisted in the production of this book – Noel and Lyn Schluter who transcribed the text from my tapes; Judy Headley for her professional editing and helpful suggestions; Irene Butte for typing the original manuscript, and for all who worked so hard to produce the first published version of *Living in the Grace of God*.

I would also like to thank everyone at Authentic for their help and assistance in producing this updated version, including all the editorial changes and additions.

Rob Rufus

Foreword

To many precious sons and daughters of God, the grace of God has been reduced either to a doctrine we talk about, or at best that by which we initially enter into a relationship with Jesus which we call salvation. Some believe that by grace we are saved by faith (see Eph. 2:8), but that after that initial entrance and beginning of the experience of salvation we are left to struggle on our own, desperately seeking to please God (and others!), but never quite making the grade. The result, of course, is a lack of joy, intimacy with the Father, and effectiveness in our witness for and service to God.

Grace isn't just the beginning, but the end as well – and everything in between! Rob Rufus has grasped this, and, over the years that we have been good friends and labourers together for Jesus, he has lived it out. I have watched the devil seek to undermine and rob him of this grace to be lived in and enjoyed but not succeed – because he has allowed the Holy Spirit to root him in it! I commend and appreciate you, Rob.

May this book get into your heart as you read, reread, study and absorb it, and enable you to enjoy all that God has richly provided for you. May you revel in the unchanging love of God, the salvation of the Lord Jesus, and the sweet fellowship of the precious Holy Spirit, all yours through this limitless grace.

Dudley Daniel

Introduction

The Extra Dimension of Grace

> So then, just as you received Christ Jesus as Lord,
> continue to live in him, rooted and built up in him,
> strengthened in the faith as you were taught, and
> overflowing with thankfulness. (Col. 2:6,7)

Grace is the extra dimension that enables us to 'live
in him'. To live in grace is to be rooted in Christ.
Grace enables us to tap into the realm of unlimited
supernatural resources. Unprecedented potential for
growth is activated in us when we live in his grace.

God's unmerited favour towards us showers us
with blessing upon blessing. We receive superior
and awesome advantages in life that cultivate in us
the full measure of the stature of Christ. Gifts, talents and abilities that would otherwise lie dormant
are suddenly released in us when we begin to flow
in grace.

God's desire for us is that we would prosper and succeed in every area of life. He wants success for us in marriage, family, finance, career, sport and recreation. Grace propels us towards this success. God does not want us to become stunted in our growth because we've allowed legalism to cut off our taproot into grace. God wants us to blossom and flourish in life, fulfilling our destiny and being fruitful.

Grace enables us to become the people we were meant to be. Many of us are tired of trying to live up to other people's expectations. It is a relief to discover that God loves us just as we are. This is unconditional love in its purest form – it's the grace of God. In this security and stability we have the freedom to grow and change, so that Christ in us is truly the hope of glory.

As you read this book and meditate on its truth, ask the Holy Spirit to help you receive grace. I am convinced that you will never be the same again.

Definition of Grace

- Grace is the divine characteristic that enables, furnishes and equips human beings to live in a supernatural dimension.
- Grace carries the refreshing reality of God's ongoing acceptance of us – an acceptance not dependent on our failures or successes.
- Grace is God's desire to bless us – not on the basis of our performance, but on the basis of Jesus' performance on our behalf.
- Grace rescues us from the syndrome of rejection and insecurity, the tyranny of performance-orientated living and the endless anxiety associated with trying to achieve and earn acceptance by keeping laws and regulations.
- Grace reveals that we are loved, valued and accepted by God as we are. Grace means that God's correction and rebuke does not involve a withdrawal of his acceptance but, rather, a proof of his love for us.

- Grace delivers us from self-effort and the heresy of the self-made person. Grace is not about what we do for God, but what God does for us.
- Grace – true grace – turns disappointment into divine appointment, and failure into a stepping stone to success.
- Grace brings the sunshine of heaven into our hearts; it releases us from the oppression of people's opinions, it nullifies Satan's accusations and it evaporates guilt and regret.
- Grace sets us free to be what God created us to be – an enthusiastic, joyful, spontaneous, unpredictable, risk-taking and secure people.

Thank God for grace!

Chapter 1

The Grace of God

The grace of God is not like old clothes that you grow out of and then throw away. Grace is something we constantly need to be reminded of, something we need to refer back to. Grace is the foundation, the platform of our lives, our ministry, our marriages – every single thing we do. We need to be living in the grace of God.

Grace – Not a Licence to Sin

Grace is not a licence to live disobediently. Living in grace gives us the capacity to obey God.

> For certain men . . . have secretly slipped in among you . . . who change the grace of our God into a licence for immorality . . .
>
> (Jude 4)

1

No, the grace of God is not a licence for sin and immorality, though there were people in Paul's day that treated it as such – and there are believers today, too, who do exactly the same thing. The grace of God ushers us into a supernatural endowment that allows us to live transcendent lives; it is what distinguishes us from those who are lost; it is what holds our marriages together; it enables us to live holy lives in intimacy with him.

Grace – Acceptance by God

Grace carries with it the revelation that you and I are accepted by God – regardless of our performance. It is the mysterious ability of God to accept us irrespective of our successes or our failures in life.

People in this world are trained to feel valuable on the basis of what they do; they live under the tyranny of their performance. Remember when you were a child and you brought your school report home, and your brother or sister achieved more that year than you? Many children feel that acceptance by their parents depends on their performance at school, and consequently feel that their successful brothers and sisters are more accepted than they are. (Wise parents accept all their children – not based on performance, but on their intrinsic value.)

Whenever I have had to discipline my children, I have impressed upon them that I love them exactly the same whether they are good or bad. My love for them is not based on their performance, but on the fact that they are my children.

We need to understand that we have value in God, irrespective of how much we are doing for God. Even if we never read the Bible again, never witness again, never pray again, never go to church again, God would love us exactly the same as if we were doing everything perfectly!

As a consequence of growing up in a world that breeds rejection, many Christians have a fragile self-image. The advertising world commercializes this insecure spirit of rejection – 'If you don't wear these clothes, or that perfume, or live in this house, or drive that car, you are not acceptable.'

There is an apostolic pattern to Paul's letters. He always begins by telling his readers how wonderful they are because of the grace of God; how they're accepted, justified, loved by God, viewed as if sinless. He lays a foundation that says, 'You are valuable, irrespective of your performance!'

Then later in the letters he says, 'Because you are accepted, because you are valuable through God's grace, throw off sin. Come on, stop doing that. Sort it out and move on in God!'

This may seem like semantics to some people, but until we get the bottom line right – that we're accepted regardless of our performance – we cannot go on to challenge other believers.

Many Christians don't want to hear another promise of victorious living, or another promise from the Scriptures of the exciting life they can experience, because in their minds they are saying, 'That's torture and torment. I can't attain that! I can't live up to that! I've tried and failed.'

But once they have the revelation 'I am accepted; even if I don't pray, I am still accepted!' they can respond to the call, 'Come on, let's pray. Let's go to the nations,' because they are not doing it to obtain God's acceptance and approval – they already have that.

The majority of Christians who backslide do so because they do not understand this bottom-line grace principle and are constantly living under a feeling of 'I am not doing enough to be accepted.'

Four things that happen if we live in the grace of God

1. We rule and reign in life

If we live in the grace of God as a lifestyle, we will rule and reign over demon powers. We will rule and reign in life.

> For if, by the trespass of the one man, death reigned through that one man, how much more will those who receive God's abundant provision of grace and of the gift of righteousness reign in life through the one man, Jesus Christ. (Rom. 5:17)

Paul's analysis of how to reign in life has nothing to do with our deeds, but everything to do with our receiving the abundance of God's grace. When we put the law on people who are already believers, we weaken them. We cripple people when we say, 'The law says in Deuteronomy 6:5, "Love the LORD your God with all your heart and with all your soul and with all your strength." Therefore LOVE GOD! Come on, how much do you love God?'

But the New Testament has nothing to do with that. 'We love because he first loved us' (1 Jn. 4:19). Loving God has nothing to do with trying to work up love for him, but it has to do with receiving his love. As we receive his love, we find the capacity to reciprocate love back to God.

There is a little switch in our spirit which has either 'transmission on' or 'reception on'. Most Christians have switched to 'transmission', so when you pray for them to receive grace they are busy trying to give to God. They don't understand that reigning in life is dependent on receiving grace from the living God.

'Let us then approach the throne of grace with confidence, so that we may receive mercy and find grace to help us in our time of need' (Heb. 4:16). It is not coming boldly to the throne room of self-achievement: 'Oh Lord, this whole week I have done nothing wrong. I've read my Bible three hours every day. I've really made it this week, so I'm coming to the throne room of self-achievement!' No, no!

'God opposes the proud but gives grace to the humble' (Jas. 4:6). Rather, we should come with this attitude: 'God, I'm coming today because I need grace.' If we ever pray with boldness because we've had a successful week, we are living on dangerous ground. We have shifted our confidence from the cross of Christ and his achievement for us to our own performance.

When we have boldness based on our performance, I guarantee we have a crisis of depression coming because our performance is by no means perfect. But we can have boldness before the throne in times of need, to obtain grace.

Christians who move their security from grace to the things they do – praying, preaching, reading the Bible, etc. – start to feel lukewarm, cold, no longer on fire for God. Until they move their security back to the grace of God they will find no joy in their salvation. By lifting the law off themselves by returning to grace, they will find the fire fanned back to life.

2. The grace of God enables us to be fruitful in life

The law cripples spiritual life, but the grace of God makes us fruitful. 'All over the world this gospel is bearing fruit and growing, just as it has been doing among you since the day you heard it and understood God's grace in all its truth' (Col. 1:6).

'Now I commit you to God and to the word of his grace, which can build you up and give you an inheritance among all those who are sanctified' (Acts 20:32). The word of grace builds us up and produces our inheritance. Without grace, prayer and fasting will not bring our inheritance, but when we are built up by grace, the inheritance of God pours in spontaneously.

3. The grace of God teaches us to say 'No' to ungodliness

The Bible says that 'sinful passions [are] aroused by the law' (Rom. 7:5). In the past, we have seen prominent Christians exposed as living in immorality. Suddenly God lifted the lid off and we saw immorality there. Somewhere, the church got it wrong.

Before they were exposed, these people were preaching legalism and criticism. The law stirs up sin! Immorality came into the church because the church had been weakened by the law. The church needs to get free from the law, grow in the grace of God, and start saying 'No' to ungodliness. The world is waiting to see a holy people emerge in this age.

> For the grace of God that brings salvation has appeared to all men. It teaches us to say 'No' to ungodliness and worldly passions, and to live

self-controlled, upright and godly lives in this pres-
ent age. (Tit. 2:11,12)

4. Grace empowers us to do great exploits for God

If we live in the true grace of God we will do more
than anyone else; we will go further for God, we
will go the second mile, we will lay down our lives.
When we are empowered by grace, we'll be ener-
gized to do great exploits for God.

> For I am the least of the apostles and do not even
> deserve to be called an apostle, because I persecuted
> the church of God. But by the grace of God I am what
> I am, and his grace to me was not without effect. No,
> I worked harder than all of them – yet not I, but the
> grace of God that was with me. (1 Cor. 15:9,10)

Grace – God Relating to Us

God always wants to relate to us on the basis of
grace. God called Abraham on the basis of grace.
'Abram believed the LORD, and he credited it to him
as righteousness' (Gen. 15:6).

Abraham went to Egypt, lied about Sarah not
being his wife and she was taken by Pharaoh.
However, God spoke to Pharaoh and warned him

that his life was at stake. So Pharaoh dismissed both Abraham and Sarah from Egypt, and they left there richer than when they had arrived.

It is not that God wants to endorse lying, but, in the grace of God, Abraham comes in and goes out having more. The blessing is not on the basis of works, but on the basis of grace.

Four hundred and thirty years after Abraham, the Mosaic Law arrived – not to replace grace, but to show us even more that we need grace! The law says: 'I will carry my end, and I will bless you if you carry your end. But if you fail, I will curse you.' Then the 'Old' arrangement was made redundant and a 'New' arrangement came in. God said: 'I will carry my end, and then I will come and carry your end, and I will treat you as if you had carried your end yourself!'

God is saying, 'I will bless you not on the basis of your performance, but on the basis of Jesus' performance on your behalf!'

This is the gospel!
This is the New Covenant!
This is grace!

Time to reflect:

- Meditate on these words: God has said: 'I will carry my end, and then I will come and carry your end, and I will treat you as if you had carried your end yourself!'

- How has this chapter challenged your concept of grace?
- Have you shifted your confidence from the cross of Christ and his achievement to your own performance? If so, talk to God about this now.

Chapter 2

God is Not Angry with Us

When we live in the grace of God we experience a creative flow, a joy, a spontaneity, and an enthusiasm for life; and – best of all – we stop trying to live up to some standard that we can never reach, free from the feeling that God is angry with us.

Under Law or Entirely Under Grace?

Do you not know, brothers – for I am speaking to men who know the law – that the law has authority over a man only as long as he lives? For example, by law a married woman is bound to her husband as long as he is alive, but if her husband dies, she is released from the law of marriage. So then, if she marries another man while her husband is still alive, she is called an adulteress. But if her husband dies, she is released from that law and is not an adulteress, even though she marries another man. (Rom. 7:1–3)

11

Christians have been released from the law!

> So, my brothers, you also died to the law through the
> body of Christ, that you might belong to another, to
> him who was raised from the dead, in order that we
> might bear fruit to God. For when we were con-
> trolled by the sinful nature, the sinful passions
> aroused by the law were at work in our bodies, so
> that we bore fruit for death. But now, by dying to
> what once bound us, we have been released from the
> law so that we serve in the new way of the Spirit, and
> not in the old way of the written code. (Rom. 7:4–6)

What Paul is saying here is that every single person
born into this world is born 'married' to the Mosaic
Law. Mosaic Law is like an overbearing husband,
who has four horrific qualities:

1. The law always accuses
   It thunders accusations: 'Stop doing that', 'Do
   this', 'Don't do that!'
2. The law never lifts a finger to help
   It stands on the side of righteousness, but will
   give us no assistance.
3. Irritatingly, the law is always right
   The law points out our faults with unfailing accu-
   racy.
4. The law will never pass away
   It's bad enough that we cannot divorce the law
   (that would be spiritual adultery), but Jesus

actually says that the law itself will never pass away (Mt. 5:18).

The law tyrannizes people. We are 'married' to a fault-finding husband, who always accuses, who never lifts a finger to help, who is always right, and who will never pass away.

The only way out, Paul says, is not that the law will die, but that we die to the law, in order that we may be married to another. Then he goes on to say we are released from the law.

Satan gets behind the law. He tyrannizes us with fear and accusations that we're not witnessing enough, we're not praying enough, we're not reading the Bible enough. We're never doing enough! We must learn this well: *The Bible says we are released from the law!*

Christians Under Law

When we come into the kingdom of God the message is preached: 'It is salvation by grace. It's free, you can't earn it, you can't boast. Come in! Jesus extends an open welcome to you.'

But then we go into a back room where the counsellors are, and they tell us, 'Right, now that you are saved, you have to do this and you have to do that. You need to pray and you need to read your Bible every day.' They put law on us from the first moment we're saved. That's the first impression we get: 'Oh I see, I'm saved by grace, but – to keep God happy with me – I've got to observe rules, regulations and laws!'

Many Christians are bound in this way, right from the beginning. In trying to live under this legalistic formula they immediately run into the question: 'How do I know when I am doing enough to keep God happy?'

They think: 'I haven't shouted at my wife this week. I did have an immoral thought, but I squashed that . . . And I did all the other things I thought I had to do. Hallelujah! I'm doing OK.' But the devil will always say, 'Oh yes, but you failed to show kindness to widows and orphans, you didn't witness to everyone at work, and you only read your Bible for two hours, not three, on Tuesday night.' Living under the law is a recipe for disaster. People under the law will never feel like they are doing enough. They can't handle the pressure, so they drift away from God. Then the church points accusing fingers at them! But those people are only suffering from their inability to keep the law. Perhaps, after years of drifting in the wilderness, feeling like God can't love them any more, they will hear a message like this and rediscover grace. 'Oh Lord Jesus, I remember. It's all by grace! Oh God, I'm coming back to you. I realize you love me irrespective of my performance. And – now that I am coming back to you – I'm not going to do this, and I'm not going to do that, but I will do this and I will do that.' And within a couple of months they are disillusioned again because they are living under the law!

Redundancy of the Law

The law is not evil, the law is good; but it has no power to give life.

> You foolish Galatians! Who has bewitched you? Before your very eyes Jesus Christ was clearly portrayed as crucified. I would like to learn just one thing from you: Did you receive the Spirit by observing the law, or by believing what you heard? Are you so foolish? After beginning with the Spirit, are you now trying to attain your goal by human effort? . . . All who rely on observing the law are under a curse, for it is written: 'Cursed is everyone who does not continue to do everything written in the Book of the Law.' (Gal. 3:1–3,10)

There is a curse that comes on people who try to live under law – be it Mosaic Law, Pentecostal law, or charismatic law. But 'Christ redeemed us from the curse of the law . . .' (Gal. 3:13a).

So then, why did God give us the law?

> Is the law, therefore, opposed to the promises of God? Absolutely not! For if a law had been given

that could impart life, then righteousness would certainly have come by the law. But the Scripture declares that the whole world is a prisoner of sin, so that what was promised, being given through faith in Jesus Christ, might be given to those who believe.

Before this faith came, we were held prisoners by the law, locked up until faith should be revealed. So the law was put in charge to lead us to Christ that we might be justified by faith. Now that faith has come, we are no longer under the supervision of the law. (Gal. 3:21–25)

Daily Living and the Law

There are times when we are not very zealous for God; we feel 'cold' spiritually. This often has nothing to do with spirituality – it's just that some days we are not at our best. There are physiological things which mean we just don't feel very spiritual. It could be because we've been working too hard, it could be that the pressures and demands are too great – we need a holiday; and there are menstrual and diurnal rhythms and cycles that can upset our balance in daily living.

Some days we just can't cope. Sometimes we have messed up, we have made mistakes, or we have just plain sinned – we feel contaminated and dirty. At that point, if we are living under the law or with a legalistic concept of God, we will go through incredible depression and a feeling of rejection.

When God disapproves of what we are doing, he does not remove his acceptance from us. The true prophetic essence of the New Testament is that when God brings rebuke, it is to comfort, exhort and to strengthen us. When God rebukes and corrects his children there comes a clear loving acceptance. He always gives us hope and a way out.

But if we are living under the law we will not hear the voice of God bringing correction, we will hear the voice of Satan condemning us.

When we have messed up, don't think the way out of that cooling-off syndrome is: 'I'd better pray more, I had better read the Bible more, I'd better do more.' That will lead to disillusionment and disaster. The way out is, 'Father, I'm feeling cool, I've messed up. I really am sorry, but I know by grace I'm accepted by you. I want to thank you that I am in Christ Jesus; I'm seated in heavenly places with you right now; even if I can't feel that, I know it's true.'

Lamb of God – Acceptable

In the Old Testament, if someone had sin in their life and they brought a lamb as a sin offering, that lamb was carefully examined by the priest (because the lamb could not be accepted if it was blind or had any kind of blemish) to see if it was acceptable.

The priest did not examine the person who brought the offering – he only examined the lamb. In the same way, our Father does not look at us, he only looks at the Lamb of God to see if that Lamb is acceptable, and – praise the Lord – Jesus is accept-able!

Blood of Jesus – Accepted

The blood of Jesus is not for our examination, but for God's! When God told Israel to put the blood of the lamb on the sides and tops of the door-frames (see Ex. 12:7), this was *outside* the house. The people were inside the house and could not touch, see or feel the blood. They could not feel the power or the effectiveness of it. But the blood was-n't for them – it was for God to examine. And when he saw it, he caused the Angel of Death to pass over.

The Accuser

In Revelation 12:10 Satan is called: '. . . the accuser of our brothers, who accuses them before our God day and night . . .' Some people think that Satan hangs around in places like Kings Cross, with all the drug addicts and prostitutes. No, that's not where Satan spends his time; rather, Satan comes to church – he spends his time with the believers, accusing them day and night. And because many believers are confused as to whether or not they are released from the law, they are vulnerable. Satan takes advantage of that.

We know that when we sin, we don't feel very good about ourselves. The answer is to quickly get back to our life-giving husband – the one who does lift a finger to help, who isn't always pointing out our faults, who doesn't constantly accuse us. He's gracious and kind and helps us – God is for us, not against us!

Many Christians are conditioned to think that when they have done something wrong, they can't worship God for at least three days. They think, 'I've got to feel really bad for three days, and then I will have earned the right to worship God boldly and come into his intimate presence again.' That's exactly what Satan wants. In those three days, while they've turned their back on God, he will take advantage of them and get them to sin again and again and again.

Detecting Legalism

Here are four simple ways to detect or discern a legalistic spirit in people.

1. They lose their sense of joy

A number of years ago I said to my wife, Glenda, 'Something's wrong in my ministry. I don't know what it is.'

She said, 'You've lost your joy. You don't enjoy it any more.'

And I realized I had come under law.

Prayer and fasting is a discipline of life and grace to me, but as soon as we make it a law, we kill the joy. I want to be with God; I enjoy being with him; but I won't be devastated if I miss a time of prayer and Bible reading. A holy discipline, yes – a legalistic, fearful bondage, no. God is not going to cause me to have an accident on the way to work if I miss my Quiet Time!

Some people are unable to worship God. They would say, 'It's just my temperament' – but it is really because they live under law. They don't feel they are worthy enough to worship God; they are bound. When people are truly released in the grace of God, one of the first things we will see is extravagant worship of the living God, because they know grace permits them to come boldly, even if they have messed up during the week.

People who can't worship are under law; they lose their joy, they live with a sense of depression, rejection, and alienation. You see, we simply cannot worship God above the level of our understanding of grace!

2. They emphasize the negative

If we ask them how they are going with their children, they will emphasize all the things that are going wrong with their kids. People who are living under grace will emphasize the things that are going well, and then (with a sense of reality) mention that there are a few small things which need to be sorted out.

3. They are insecure, jealous, competitive, threatened – they take everything personally

People under law are bound by a spirit of rejection and they try to tie up others in Pharisaical bondage. They're touchy and competitive – they hate to see other people succeed, because that threatens them.

We must learn that we are more important than anything we can do or achieve in life. We are not the sum total of our achievements. If people only love us for what we can do for them, we're better off without them. We must understand that God accepts us, and we can be truly free.

4. They are easily manipulated

Legalistic people are so desperate for acceptance they will look to anybody – even if they have to compromise truth – to receive reassurance.

A homosexual man once said to me that he would love to become a Christian, except for the fact that he felt such acceptance in the gay bars. People who do not know the grace of God will compromise to gain acceptance.

Once we know the grace of God, we live free and we will set other people free. The answer to sin is not to preach more law, but to preach more of the grace of God.

Colour Inside

There is so much colour
inside you and me,
I wonder why
we keep it in.
Isn't this grey world
dying for lack of it,
like a deprived desert
cracking in pain.
Why do we cringe
in the corridors
of conformity,
like timid little souls?
'What will people
think of us?'
are the shackles
that bind us.
As we carry our weighted
chains with earnest but fading

strength, along the dismal
pathways we tread.
Routine is the rut
that fear demands we tread,
while freedom beckons
like a lover.
But, like slaves to pretence
we say, 'We're doing fine.'
Tradition keeps us
toeing the line.
And then I see the carpenter,
dancing on the water
then I see the carpenter,
turning water into wine –
colours flashing in his presence,
chains snapping in his presence.
There is so much colour
inside you and me,
I wonder why
we keep it in.

Rob Rufus

Time to reflect:

- Meditate on these words: 'The priest did not examine the person who brought the offering – he only examined the lamb.'
- We have read that the priest didn't look at the person who made the sin offering, but the offering itself. Likewise, our heavenly Father does not

look at us – he looks at the Lamb to see if he is acceptable. And, of course, he is! How does this speak to you personally?

- If you feel it's apt, pray: 'Father . . . I have messed up. I really am sorry, but I know by grace I'm accepted by you. I want to thank you that I am in Christ Jesus; I'm seated in heavenly places with you right now; even if I can't feel that, I know it's true.'

Chapter 3

Reigning in Life

The reason why people keep the creative life of God locked inside is because they are oppressed by legalism, guilt and the accusations of Satan.

In the church today, we can hear messages that do not convey the true grace of God. Jesus said that we can know a prophet by their fruits; in the same way, we can discern a message by the fruits of that message. If it's an authentic message from our Father, the living God, the fruit of that message will be a desire to draw closer to Jesus. It will put zeal and creativity and joy in our hearts.

> For the kingdom of God is not a matter of eating and drinking, but of righteousness, peace and joy in the Holy Spirit. (Rom. 14:17)

If those fruits don't come into our lives when we hear preaching, we must judge that word as a mixed message that does not contain grace from God.

Many of us have difficulty accepting the full grace of God. We are more comfortable with a little bit of grace and a little bit of condemnation – after all, life should be miserable now and again on account of our sin! We have to learn to give our hearts and minds permission to enjoy living, to enjoy God and enjoy his grace.

Grace – Living in a Battle Zone

Life is difficult. There are landmines out there; there are fields of disaster; we are caught up in a crisis. This world is involved in the agony of cataclysmic clashes between divine and demonic forces. We're not in heaven yet, we're not in paradise – we're in a war zone! There is a supernatural clash occurring about us. There are enemy forces wanting to distract people, to take them off course away from Jesus, and send them to hell.

The apostle Paul experienced life in the battle zone – he was beaten, rejected and betrayed. Churches he planted were hijacked by legalists; he was misunderstood and misrepresented. He went through things that very few of us have ever experienced, and he prayed, 'Oh God, get this messenger of Satan away from me. Stop him from buffeting me day and night!' Three times he prayed this way, and God said to him, 'My grace is sufficient for you, for my power is made perfect in weakness' (2 Cor. 12:9).

To live in grace doesn't mean that life is always going to be nice around us, that everyone is going to treat us kindly, and all our desires will simply fall into place. But the grace of God will enable us – even in the midst of stress and pressures – to enjoy intimacy and celebrate life with Jesus Christ.

Strengthened by Grace

'Do not be carried away by all kinds of strange teachings. It is good for our hearts to be strengthened by grace, not by ceremonial foods, which are of no value to those who eat them' (Heb. 13:9). The writer to the Hebrews is saying that there are many strange teachings in Christian circles – don't be sidetracked by these things but, rather, let your hearts be strengthened by grace. There are so many pressures and stresses in our lives and we need our hearts strengthened by God's grace to live successfully.

Let us sift, filter and censor our spiritual diets. Let's not listen to people who teach legalism. I am very careful what I lend my ears to. Are you? There is an anointing within Christians that discerns when error is being taught. 'As for you, the anointing you received from him remains in you, and you do not need anyone to teach you' (1 Jn. 2:27).

The Spirit within us reacts to the teaching of error – let us be alert to that and not carried away by strange teachings. Let our hearts be strengthened by grace!

Reigning in Life Through Grace

Reigning in life is a matter of receiving grace (see Rom. 5:17, quoted earlier). We do not reign and rule in life by what we do for God, nor by keeping laws.

The devil will try to short circuit the supply of grace to our lives, because once he can do that we will be crippled – unable to reign and rule.

Law through Moses, grace through Jesus

The law was given through Moses, but grace came through Jesus Christ (see Jn. 1:17). As Moses came down the mountain with the two tablets of stone, he saw that the people below were worshipping a golden calf. On the day that the law arrived, at Moses' command, 3,000 people were executed for their sin (see Ex. 32:28).

When grace arrived on the Day of Pentecost, Peter came down from the upper room to announce the New Covenant. He didn't say, 'We're scrapping the Old Testament laws and bringing in some New Testament laws.' No, he came down with grace. And the people below were not worshipping a golden calf – they had just done something far worse, they had crucified the Lord of Glory. But the Bible says that on that Day of Pentecost, 3,000 of them were saved!

Why People Resist Grace

We are all either receiving grace, or we are actively resisting grace. There are at least three reasons why people resist grace.

1. People have not dealt adequately with their guilt and their shame
   If you scratch below the surface of many Christians, you will find they are far better acquainted with their failures, their guilt and their shame than they are with the character of the God of grace. Their sin is more real to them than any intimate familiarity with the living God. But we have to understand we are all unworthy. And our unworthiness has been dealt with permanently by the grace of God. If we fail to come to terms with that fact, we will end up resisting the grace of God.
2. People think that grace puts them in debt to God
   There is a teaching which says that if Jesus was God, and he died on the cross for me, then I owe him everything. If we owe God for what Jesus did on the cross, it wasn't grace, it was a bargain: 'I'll do this for you, if you'll do that for me.'

Grace means we are not in debt, but we have to give our minds permission to believe that. Yes, we are thankful, and we are full of gratitude to God. But we cannot 'pay him back' for what he has done. If people believe they are in debt to God, they will spend their lives trying to pay him back and will move, in a subtle fashion, into a life of self-works. They will lose their capacity to go on a holiday or to relax in any way, because of the conviction that they should be out on the street witnessing twenty-four hours a day!

3. Pride keeps people from receiving grace

When Jesus, who was grace itself, came to Peter and said, 'Let me wash your feet,' Peter resisted grace in the strongest terms possible. On the same occasion, Peter was so full of himself and his own ability that he vowed and declared he would follow Jesus anywhere. Yet within a few hours he denied three times that he had even heard of Jesus. If feet are dirty, and grace offers to wash them, feet must receive grace!

False pride disguises and camouflages its self-sufficiency and independence, but when grace *offers* we say, 'Lord, I receive.'

The Need to Receive

When we learn how to receive grace, then we will rule and reign in life.

The thief who hung on the cross next to Jesus said, 'Jesus, remember me when you come into your kingdom' (Lk. 23:42). Jesus did not tell him that he should first have kept a whole lot of laws and got holy enough. Instead he turned to him and said, 'Today you will be with me in paradise' (Luke 23:43).

This man was a criminal dying for his crimes and he knew that he was desperately in need of grace. We need God's grace just as desperately as that thief, but we are not always aware of it.

The Time to Receive

We should not wait for the grace of God to come into our lives, asking only when we are under hardship, pressure and difficulties. The time to receive grace is when things are going well. We need to learn how to receive grace for the ability to live our everyday lives. I have said before that most Christians have switched to 'transmission' – they are busy trying to give to God. Many people are trained how to transmit through their spiritual antennae, but they don't know how to switch over to 'reception' and receive the tangible grace of God.

You know, people who are able to receive this supernatural empowering flowing tangibly into their lives don't always need other people to encourage them. They are able to encourage themselves in the Lord and even under the most extreme pressures they can rise up and release other people from captivity.

If we receive grace, we will rule and reign over temptation, demons, accusations, gloom and condemnatory depression.

Channels of Grace

The first channel of grace is *faith*. Romans 5:2 says, 'through whom we have gained access by faith into this grace in which we now stand. And we rejoice in the hope of the glory of God.'

We gain access into the grace of God through faith. Faith is not a psychological positive thinking phenomenon. Faith is a supernatural force that operates from our inner being – it flows from our spirit. When we have a revelation by faith of the grace of God, we can draw the grace of God into our lives.

Many people in Christian circles have head knowledge of the grace of God as an academic truth better than I could ever teach it. They think they can sit around and grace will just mysteriously work into their being without them doing anything! However, grace comes in reality through particular ordained channels and if God's people don't get themselves under those channels to receive grace, they will never walk in the blessings of the grace of

God. So, faith is the vehicle that brings us into the blessings of God.

The second channel of grace is a *humble heart*. James 4:6 says, 'God opposes the proud but gives grace to the humble.'

We must be careful to distinguish between true humility and false humility. True humility is when we know how to receive a compliment, but in our hearts we say, 'Father, I thank you for your grace to do this thing well.' False humility says, 'I'm not very good really, I just get by.'

Of course we are all unworthy, but God gives us the grace to rise above it. The truly humble heart, when faced with a challenge, prays, 'Jesus, help me! God, I need your grace.' Without God's grace we cannot do anything supernatural that will last for eternity.

We have to have faith and believe we can receive grace. We have to humble our hearts and be dependent on God. It is actually the weak who rule and reign and succeed in the kingdom of God. Why? Because the weak are humble and God gives them grace.

The third channel of grace is *a true revelation of the character of God*. Most of us from a very young age have been conditioned through the media, our culture and through religion to have distorted misconceptions of the character of God. God's Word says in 2 Peter 1:2, 'Grace and peace be yours in abundance through the knowledge of God and of Jesus our Lord.' God promises that grace will come in abundance if we know what he is like. The more we understand the true character of God, the more grace begins to flow in our lives.

That is why Satan loves to distort the character of God more than anyone or anything. Whenever he can, he attacks the integrity and character of God. He injects suspicion about the grace of God.

Breaking Down Strongholds

The strongholds that need to be broken down are our thought patterns. When we believe the lies of Satan about the character of God, strongholds are established in our minds. These erroneous concepts about God cause us to resist the grace of God.

In Genesis chapter 3 we read how Satan caused Eve to sin. It was not just by the power of temptation, because she had grace enough to resist. But once Satan undermined the integrity of God's character, Eve was instantly vulnerable to fall.

He created suspicion in her mind that caused an internal dialogue of confusion in her thinking. Satan took the one restriction that God had placed on Adam and Eve (not to eat of the tree of the knowledge of good and evil), focused on it, and created suspicion about God's motives (he doesn't want you to be like him).

Eve entered into what we can never afford to enter into; an internal dialogue with her own mind saying, 'I wonder if maybe that is why God doesn't want me to eat of that fruit, because he doesn't want me to become like him.'

We, like Eve, can develop in our thinking processes strongholds about the knowledge of God. Some people have suffered at the hands of a violent father. This gives them a distorted idea of God. Others have good fathers who provide well for them but are so busy that they don't have time to spend with their children. The children grow up feeling that they weren't important enough to warrant Dad's attention. When our earthly fathers fall short, our image of our heavenly Father falls short as well.

These strongholds in our thinking must be pulled down! In 2 Corinthians 10:4, Paul tells us: 'The weapons we fight with are not the weapons of the world. On the contrary, they have divine power to demolish strongholds.' And to show that these strongholds are in our minds, 2 Corinthians 10:5 says, 'We demolish arguments and every pretension that sets itself up against the knowledge of God, and we take captive every thought to make it obedient to Christ.'

Once the strongholds are broken down, we need to fill our hearts and minds with the truth of God's Word. God's character is wonderfully revealed in Ephesians 1.

Chosen, Adopted and Accepted

In this first chapter of Ephesians, Paul tells us that before the beginning of time and before the creation of the world, God the Father chose us and adopted us according to his good pleasure. There was nothing in and of ourselves to merit being chosen, but he chose us just the same. Then he adopted us and accepted us in 'the beloved' (KJV) – that is, in Christ Jesus – according to the glorious grace that he lavished on us.

Many Christians mentally understand that they are chosen and adopted by God, but they have no revelation that they are accepted in the beloved.

When the Father was choosing us, he saw that we had a birth defect through Adam's fall. When the Father brought us to salvation, he said in his mercy and his compassion, 'I see that you are still deformed; that you still cry out in the night even though you are grown men and women. I still see in the darkness of your circumstances. In the nightmare and the horror of the darkness in this world, and in the desperate times when you cry out, I will be right there to comfort you. I will treat you as one of my very own children. The proof of this is that I signed your adoption papers in the blood of my Son. You are accepted in the beloved.'

That is the grace of God! When we come into the kingdom, we are chosen and adopted. We are not on probation. We are accepted just as we are for eternity. We have to give our minds permission to believe that this is the truth.

As A.W. Tozer says[1]

> We, as Christians, instinctively try to be like our God. If we conceive him to be stern and exacting, we will be that way ourselves. From a failure to properly understand God comes a world of unhappiness among good Christians.
>
> The Christian life is thought to be gloom; unrelieved cross carrying life under the eye of a stern God who expects much and excuses nothing. He is austere, peevish, highly temperamental and extremely hard to please.
>
> The kind of life that springs out of such libellous notions must of necessity be but a parody of the true life in Christ.
>
> It is most important to our spiritual welfare that we always hold in our minds a right concept of God. If we think of him as cold and exacting, we shall find it impossible to love him and our lives will be ridden with servile fear. If again we hold him to be kind and understanding, our whole inner life will mirror that idea.

God's True Character

Tozer goes on to say

> The truth is that God is the most winsome of all beings and his service one of unspeakable pleasure.

He is all love and those who trust him need never know anything but that love.

He will not condone sin, but through the blood of his everlasting covenant he is able to act toward us exactly as if we had never sinned.

For the trusting sons of men his mercy will always triumph over justice. The fellowship of God is delightful. He communes with his redeemed ones in an easy uninhibited fellowship that is restful and healing to the soul. He is not over sensitive or selfish or temperamental. He is easy to please and loves us unconditionally. He expects of us only what he himself has first supplied.

He is quick to overlook imperfections. He loves us for ourselves and values our love more than galaxies of new created worlds.

How good it would be if we could learn that God is easy to live with; he remembers our frame and knows that we are dust.

He may sometimes chasten us, it is true, but even this he does with a smile, the proud tender smile of a father who is bursting with pleasure over an imperfect but promising son, who is coming every day to look more and more like the one whose child he is.

I believe that it can take years of being exposed to the truth about God's character until our minds are fully released from the erroneous concepts of God.

When we do come to understand that we are loved irrespective of our actions, we will realize that he sees us as worthwhile of his devoted, specific attention on a daily basis. When we have a revelation of this truth, we can come boldly to the throne room of grace to find in abundance the grace that we need.

Time to reflect:

- Meditate on these words: 'When we learn how to receive grace, then we will rule and reign in life.'
- Read 2 Corinthians 12:9. How will receiving the grace of God help us when life gets tough?
- How can we grow in a true understanding of the character of God? Pray: 'Father, thank you that you reveal your true character in your Word. Thank you that your Son makes you known to us, for he is the exact representation of your being. Help me to focus today on who you *really* are. Amen.'

Chapter 4

Grace Haters

I cannot teach on the grace of God without addressing those who oppose grace. Grace is awesome in its power to change lives. But radical change encounters radical opposition. It is therefore not surprising that we have to deal with the grace haters.

Grace haters are the legalists who will try to intimidate, manipulate and dominate people with a spirit of witchcraft. The religious spirit in them wants everyone stereotyped and conformed to their own bondage. They are parrots and puppets, no longer voices for God, but echoes, not pursuing God but pursuing opportunities for position and prestige. They are cloned to act the same, dress the same and speak in the same religious tones. You know, where everyone looks the same you can be sure a religious spirit is operating!

If you try to live in the grace of God, I guarantee Satan will send his agent across your path to try to intimidate you and insinuate that you ought not to be living the way you are, that your freedom is not freedom but licentiousness. If you haven't experienced this sort of thing it's probably because you have never lived in grace.

Jesus: the Manifestation of Grace

In the New Testament, if you look at Jesus you see the very manifestation of grace itself. By contrast, the spirit of religion is manifested in the Pharisees.

Everywhere Jesus went the sinners loved him because he gave redemptive life. The Pharisees, on the other hand, hated him. They hated him so much that they tried to kill him because he broke the Sabbath and made himself equal with God, calling God his Father (see Jn. 5:18).

John chapter 5 tells the story of the man who had been crippled for thirty-eight years. Jesus told him, 'Get up! Pick up your mat and walk' (Jn. 5:8). He was not worried about it being the Sabbath because he was more concerned about setting the man free. The Pharisees, however, were very concerned to see this man walking through the streets carrying his bed. They were preoccupied with their petty concerns over him breaking the Sabbath, rather than rejoicing with him over the miracle he had received; to the Pharisees, the law was more important than people.

Their response to Jesus was 'How dare you?' But Jesus was unperturbed. He maintained his grace perspective, telling them, 'My Father is always at his work to this very day, and I, too, am working' (Jn. 5:17).

Jesus did not reject the law; he interpreted the law through the eyes of grace.

The Legalistic Religious Spirit

What do you think about when you think of 'religion' – Hinduism, Buddhism, Islam . . . or some of the more 'traditional' Christian denominations? Did you know the church of Jesus Christ has been infiltrated by spirits of religion and legalism that masquerade as the authentic, but actually hinder millions of people from pouring into the kingdom of God?

When the person Jesus Christ walked on this earth, people by the thousands poured in to be in his presence. When the church of Jesus Christ arises to the full measure of the stature of Christ and shakes off religiosity and legalism, the world will beat a pathway to get into the churches and stand in the sparkling beauty of grace. The prophetic church is not aggressive, haughty or arrogant, but speaks the truth in love and sets people free. And we do have to be truthful. We try to be nicer than Jesus instead of dealing radically with the religious spirit! Jesus referred to the Pharisees as a 'brood of vipers' and 'whitewashed tombs'.

Paul, the apostolic man who wrote three-quarters of the New Testament, wrote to the Galatians in very strong terms, warning them of the dangers of the religious spirit. We read in Galatians 1:7: 'Evidently some people are throwing you into confusion and are trying to pervert the gospel of Christ.' This was a very strong charge to bring against people – that they were 'trying to pervert the gospel'. Again in Galatians 2:4, he referred to 'false brothers' who 'infiltrated our ranks to spy on the freedom we have in Christ Jesus and to make us slaves.' His motive for clearly exposing this falsehood is seen in Galatians 2:5: 'We did not give in to them for a moment, so that the truth of the gospel might remain with you.' Paul's desire was purely to protect the freedom of others.

Paul was so committed to the truth that he was not afraid to confront Peter when he compromised his freedom. In Galatians 2:11 he wrote, 'When Peter came to Antioch, I opposed him to his face, because he was clearly in the wrong.' Paul must have been a very secure man. He saw how Peter ate with the Gentiles, but when certain men came from James, Peter drew back and separated himself because he was afraid (Gal. 2:12). Peter's fear also led others astray as we see in Galatians 2:13.

Paul was opposing the effects of the religious spirit in operation. He did not want the people to lose their freedom. So in Galatians 2:21 he said, 'I do not set aside the grace of God, for if righteousness could be gained through the law, Christ died for nothing!'

Paul knew that religion was a burden. Religious people have no joy and carry big burdens around with them. They are bad adverts for a lost world. People in the world have their own burdens and try to escape through pleasure in sin. Their sin only increases their burdens and doesn't provide the relief they are looking for. They need to find a people with a liberty of living in God's grace. Galatians 5:1 says, 'It is for freedom that Christ has set us free. Stand firm, then, and do not let yourselves be burdened again by a yoke of slavery.'

Paul dealt radically with the deception of the religious spirit. He addressed those who were preaching circumcision and thereby robbing others of their freedom in Christ by saying, 'You who are trying to be justified by law have been alienated from Christ; you have fallen away from grace' (Gal. 5:4). He had a radical suggestion for them: 'As for those agitators, I wish they would go the whole way and emasculate themselves!' (v.12). Paul would rather they cut the whole thing off than put others under the bondage of the law of circumcision.

Misguided religious zeal

I believe that the most obnoxious destructive force in the world today is misguided religious zeal. I'm not just talking about the dangers of terrorism post 9/11 – *millions* have died in religious wars throughout the centuries because of misguided, perverted religious zeal.

Paul had been trained all his life in law. From a young age he was taught by some of the best rabbis and teachers in Israel. He was very ambitious, very zealous and very committed to the traditions and religious laws that had been ingrained into him. So zealous was he that he persecuted and executed Christians wherever he went. But it took only one brief supernatural encounter with the living Christ and Paul was transformed from a misguided religious zealot into a humble, passionate man of God with a heart after the truth of Jesus Christ.

There is hope for all of us. God isn't into delivering sermons; he is into delivering people. If someone as religious and legalistic as Paul can be delivered, anyone can!

When people who have had religious bondage in their lives get set free by grace, they become the most wonderfully committed people of God and will never again allow others to put them back into bondage. This is what happened to me. I got saved out of the Hare Krishna movement, where I practiced a level of legalism and religiosity that is unmatched in the Christian church. Now if a legalistic Christian comes to me with the attitude that they are keeping all these laws and I am just some floppy charismatic, something in me says, 'You've

come too late! I have already been far more religious than you could ever imagine. I've tried
religion and it doesn't bring you any closer to God.'

Now I am determined to never again let anyone
ever pull me away from the intimacy I have with God
through grace!

Reality

When legalists come to us there is a demeanour and
a posture about them that is intimidating because
they look like they have got it all together. They
don't have it all together in reality, but they give the
impression that they do! With some, it is the way
they carry their Bibles. With others, it is their pious
tone of voice. However, their outward show of
piety is lacking in reality. They will never let you
know if they have sinned. They will never be vulnerable, honest and open. You cannot replace intimacy with God with religiosity.

Have you ever been with people who change
when they get into a religious context? Suddenly
they start looking different; their faces and body
postures change. Then when they go to say The
Grace their voices change too. They say, 'We are
going to have a meal. Let's pray. . . Oooohhh God!
We thank thee for thy bounty, which thou dost
bestow on us.'

Now, people don't normally talk like that! I don't
come to my wife and say, 'Oooohhh Glenda!' It's

not reality! So why should I come to God, who is total integrity and truth, and say, 'Oooohhh God!'? You may think that this is a trivial point – just splitting hairs. But it is stopping thousands of people from coming into the kingdom.

We need to get released from an artificial, pre-empted exaggeration of sincerity. Let's not be 'religious people'. Let's be real!

Manipulative pressure

Legalistic people try to make us feel that we should be more like them, don't they? They are preoccupied with external things and when we are around them we start to think, 'If I was more like them and didn't do this and didn't do that I would be more holy.'

There is a manipulative pressure on people to let go of grace and conform. People feel the pressure to wear the same clothes and cut their hair the same way. They begin to think that if they could just become a holy clone they could overcome their problems and struggles with life. They're in danger of getting haughty, arrogant and proud. They get caught up in mindless religious ritualism and become judgemental and critical. And worst of all, they try to make others just like them! If someone resists their manipulation, they pour guilt and condemnation on them.

I watched a prostitute be interviewed once. The interviewer asked, 'Were you ever interested in church?' She replied, 'I tried it once, but they laid too much guilt on me.' My heart broke for her. The prostitutes followed Jesus and got released when they were in his company, but the church lays guilt on them!

A Community of Grace

Some years ago, I was walking through the streets of Hong Kong with a friend of mine from South Africa. As we walked through the red light district some prostitutes came up to us and tried to solicit us. At first I felt outraged that they would approach me, a 'holy man of God'. Then God whispered in my heart, 'Show grace to the next one.' So when the next one approached me with her pimp, I said, 'How much do you charge?' My friend's eyes nearly popped out of his head as he asked himself, 'Has Rob gone over the edge? Has it all got too much for him?'

She named her price. Without batting an eyelid I said, 'That's not enough. You should charge more than that. That's too low a price. Jesus paid so much for you that he gave everything he had. He gave his life for you.'

The woman just looked at me. Her pimp grabbed her arm and started pulling her away, screaming at me in Chinese. Although I didn't understand the language, I knew he wasn't complimenting me! As he was pulling her away, the woman looked in my face.

'I knew him once,' she said.

I guarantee you that at one time that woman went to a legalistic religious church.

Am I endorsing prostitution? Of course not! Jesus would never do that. But there is a place to show grace to people so that redemptive life can flow. We need to fight the religious spirit so that people like that prostitute can come into the church. I want to see churches planted all over the world where people can come in and find grace.

The people who live in the grace of God are people who learn to love one another and accept one another. Church becomes family when we live in the grace of God. People living in the grace of God pray for one another more, reach out to the lost more and value people more. They start feeding the hungry, clothing the poor and going amongst the broken street people restoring dignity to them. They go beyond the walls of their building to infiltrate the world and mix with sinners. They help those who are sick. They know it is not the Christian's job to judge whether the illnesses people suffer from are what they deserve. None of us deserve salvation. Just because someone is dying of a disease like Aids doesn't make them any less deserving of salvation! We must show non-judgemental love and mercy to a sick and dying world.

If, after receiving grace, people still sin continually and refuse to be disciplined, then the process of biblical judgement must come. There is a place for that, but it is a rare extreme case. We must keep uppermost in our minds the truth that the church is a community of grace.

We must not be intimidated by the legalists at any time. We must not underestimate the power of their deception and fear, but we must never give in to it. Radical change encounters radical opposition, but grace will always win!

Time to reflect:

- Meditate on these words: 'If you look at Jesus you see the very manifestation of grace itself.'
- How can we tell if there is a legalistic religious spirit operating in us – or in our church community?
- Read Luke 7:36–50. Then pray: 'Father, help me to be real. And help me to treat every person I meet with grace – just like your Son.'

Chapter 5

Guilt

There is a phenomenon in the world today that is far more lethal and destructive than Aids and cancer put together. It is attacking every one of us on a daily basis. This phenomenon is the weight of oppressive guilt – guilt that God never intended for us nor designed us to cope with. Even a little bit of guilt is a total overload to the system of humankind that results in all kinds of psychosomatic diseases and disorders.

Guilt has the power to paralyze the people of God. The goal of the Holy Spirit is to teach us to shake off oppressive guilt that comes from the enemy.

Guilt: an Inadequate Motivator

Some people will say, 'If I don't feel guilt, how will I ever be motivated?' This is a big problem. When you take away guilt (motivation for many Christians) they are suddenly lost and they don't know how to follow Jesus. But when guilt is the motivation for action, good intentions don't last.

When people pray or do good works because they feel guilty, they can only keep it up for a few weeks or a few months at the most. I want to tell you why there is so much fickleness, unfaithfulness and lack of commitment and zeal in the body of Christ. It is because too many people think that guilt motivation is what Christianity is all about – and that is why the church is weak. People under guilt think that when you preach grace it is a licence to sin and do what you want. They lack consistency, determination, endurance and perseverance. They back off at the slightest difficulty, opposition, betrayal or disappointment.

Get Motivated by Grace!

When we truly understand grace, we will lay down our lives passionately, zealously, faithfully and totally to follow Jesus enthusiastically even if it means at any cost, at any price. When we live under grace we can keep doing this for sixty or seventy years non-stop. God wants us to be drawn by grace, not driven by guilt. He wants us to get released from religious routines and move into grooves of grace that will propel us forward.

We have to learn to shake off guilt that is latent in our minds, in our emotions and in our cultural conditioning. There is so much of it in our lives that we are not even aware of it. God gave me a picture of the church needing to vigorously and systematically shake off the chains of guilt that are causing psychosomatic diseases, psychological disorientation and confusion. We must be free and liberated in the grace of God so that we can

- win our neighbourhoods
- win our cities and
- win the nations for God

A grace-orientated and motivated people are zealous, fresh and passionate for Jesus Christ.

Godly Sorrow/Worldly Sorrow

We have already seen that Satan is 'the accuser of our brothers, who accuses them before our God day and night' (Rev. 12:10). Christians are under a twenty-four hour attack from Satan to accuse and bring oppressive guilt.

The oppressive guilt that results from Satan's accusations brings worldly sorrow, not godly sorrow. We must learn to distinguish between the two.

Godly sorrow comes when we realize we are doing something wrong, sinning and disobeying

God. As Paul says in 2 Corinthians 7:10: 'Godly sorrow brings repentance that leads to salvation and leaves no regret, but worldly sorrow brings death.' Godly sorrow comes when

- we have lost our zeal
- we are just going through religious routines
- we are half-hearted
- we are compromising on the sidelines
- we are hiding bitterness in our hearts
- we have immorality hidden somewhere in secret places

When that is our state, the Holy Spirit comes to help us. He loves us so much he will come and convict us of sin. He will not come to condemn, threaten or intimidate us. He will come and break our hearts with the loveliness of God. We will sense by revelation the goodness of our God and it will lead us to repentance when we see how great, good and merciful God is. Our hearts will be broken with grief when we see the sin we are doing and realize that we have hurt God. Everything in our being will be motivated positively to change and get rid of wrong in our lives.

Godly sorrow brings change for the better, but worldly sorrow brings psychological guilt that is demotivating, destructive and paralyzing. It causes disease in the church and does not come from the Holy Spirit but from our enemy the devil. God is too wise to motivate with psychological guilt or worldly sorrow because he knows it triggers four things in us

- fear of punishment
- loss of self-esteem
- depression
- feelings of isolation and rejection

When people are living under psychological guilt they are living under the suppression of worldly sorrow which they think is God. They feel stressed, pressurized, discouraged and oppressed with guilt. They are deceived into believing it is the voice of God, but I want to tell you that demonic depressive guilt is never the voice of God. The devil is the Christian's accuser and Jesus is the 'one who speaks to the Father in our defence' (1 Jn. 2:1). He is our lawyer, our counsel or advocate for our defence. When we sin he is not there to condemn us, but to lift us up and help us move on in holiness.

When the enemy comes to accuse us we need to receive grace on a daily basis to overcome discouragement. Hebrews 11:6 says, 'He rewards those who earnestly seek him.' When we look to God daily we pick up the inspiration and motivation of his grace. When we don't look to God to receive grace on a daily basis, we get into guilt.

There are five guilt games that people play when they give way to discouragement:

1. They give up and suffer depression and self-pity.
2. They rebel and fight back by doing even more wrong.
3. They refuse to acknowledge any blame whatsoever for their own state and project it onto everyone and everything else. They criticize the faults of others as they try to hide their guilt.
4. They superficially acknowledge their faults without any sincerity saying, 'I can't win anyway' and 'Yes, I am wrong anyway.' There is no godly sorrow that leads to repentance, just worldly sorrow with a superficial repentance that continues in disobedience.
5. They are driven with perfectionist idealism that is far-fetched and unreasonable. Their reasoning is this: 'I am so sick and tired of feeling guilty about my wrongs. If the only way to gain self-respect and respect from God and people is to be perfect, then perfect I will be.' They are a pain to be with, lose friends and eventually lose contact with people.

How does this oppressive guilt start in our lives? I want to use two psychological words here – ideal self and punitive self.

The ideal self

The ideal self is something that is formed on the inside of every one of us in our pre-adolescent years. By the time we reach adolescence we have a concept on the inside of us of our ideal self. It is formed by the influence of parents, teachers, peers and miscellaneous authority figures, people we respect and even some harsh, insensitive authority figures.

This ideal self on the inside of us will vary from society to society. We have a picture inside of what we think we should be. Our ideal self may not reflect a biblical picture. Some people's ideal self allows them to go and have sexual intercourse with as many people as they want. That is definitely not God's plan for them. Then again, some people's ideal self won't buy toothpaste that is advertised using sex appeal. It makes them feel guilty.

Ghetto children in South Africa are taught by their parents to fight for their rights and be aggressive. In other societies, parents discourage aggression and teach compliance and conformity. So from society to society, people have different ideal selves. Nevertheless, whenever they fall below the concept of their ideal selves they feel guilt and that is when the punitive self leaps into action.

The punitive self

The punitive self develops intricate ways of inflicting punishment on us for falling below our ideal self. It comes into action when we fall below our picture of the ideal self, even though most times that ideal self has nothing to do with biblical truth.

When we do wrong, our punitive self begins to say things like, 'You should be ashamed of yourself', 'You're bad', 'How could God love you?' and 'You're nothing!' Then it begins to inflict intricate forms of punishment. For example, when people suffer from anorexia and bulimia it can be seen as a blatant form of the punitive self trying to punish the person for falling below their ideal self. The perfectionist punitive self says, 'You are falling below, you are too fat', and it comes to inflict punishment.

There are even more sinister ways that people punish themselves. Some people gravitate towards failure on purpose because they feel they don't deserve success in life. They must punish themselves because they are so far below their ideal self. They deliberately sabotage their own success; they cannot allow themselves to experience pleasure or to enjoy life in any way. Deep depression and suicidal tendencies can be the result.

Grace releases us from guilt

We need revelation from God to know how much there is a punitive self that is trying to tyrannize us. The grace of God has to come and release us. So, if we want to overcome self-indulgence and get delivered from the ideal self and the punitive self so that we don't live under guilt, we need to

- have intimacy with God
- focus on God
- have a flow of grace from God

Understanding Discipline

We must learn to discern between God's punishment and his discipline. If we fail to differentiate, we will crumble under the weight of guilt. There are certain passages in the Bible that make us think, 'My God! Are you like that?'

We need to realize that in this world people do wrong and they deserve punishment. When someone kills another human being they deserve to be punished. We can't have chaos.

Now, God has every right to punish wrongdoing fully. So when we read those scriptures that promise us horrendous punishment, we shrivel up because we know that is what we deserve. But that is the wonder of the gospel! Jesus came and took

- all the anger
- all the wrath
- all the punishment of God in our place

Therefore, God has no punishment left for us. For the person who is in Christ, the wrath of God's punishment has burnt itself out on the innocent head of Jesus Christ and there is only God's loving discipline left – discipline that will bring us to maturity in Jesus. Consequently, the safest place to be in the universe is in Christ.

- Punishment is for the purpose of justice, to inflict penalty for an offence. Punishment is payback for wrongs done. That is what God did to Jesus on the cross for you and me.
- Discipline is for the purpose of maturing us, to correct us and to promote positive growth. That is what God does for us.
- Punishment focuses on the past things that we have done and reflects God's anger.
- Discipline focuses on the future and reflects God's love.
- Punishment produces fear, guilt, hostility and anxiety.
- Discipline produces security.

We need to understand that all our wrong has been *fully* punished. The trouble with us is that we live in a time/space world. We don't understand the eternal dimension, so when we do something wrong, we think God wants to punish us and he is angry with us. But he is not angry with us, because he has already been angry with us and punished us 2,000 years ago! We must clearly see that now all he has left to deal with is to bring discipline, correction and adjustment to bring us to maturity – and he does it with love.

The legacy of earthly parents

We have to understand that our earthly parents (or whoever cared for us as children) did not discipline us in the way that God disciplines us.

There is a psychological root that is deep in our souls from the way we were brought up; we have ingrained into us the belief that when we do wrong we first get punished and then we get disciplined. After the penalty the correction came. I believe most of our parents did this to greater or lesser degrees. But now we are in the kingdom of God and when we do wrong we don't get punished because God has already punished Jesus in our place. Only discipline comes. So we get a bit insecure; we have been programmed by our own upbringing to expect punishment. We go around wrongly assuming that maybe God is accumulating punishment for us!

Rejection

A lot of God's people need God's discipline because they are in disorder and are disobedient. But if they don't understand the difference between punishment and discipline, when the discipline comes they will take it as rejection and withdraw saying, 'I am going to leave and go to another church now!' because they think rebuke is rejection. But God wants us to know that discipline is not rejection.

Recognizing judgement

If people keep on repeatedly resisting God's discipline, there is a time in extreme cases where God will bring his judgement (1 Cor. 5:5 ff.; Acts 5:1–11).

Paul told the Corinthian church to 'Expel the wicked man from among you' (1 Cor. 5:13) when he wrote to them about a man who was sleeping with his father's wife. He said, 'hand this man over to Satan, so that the sinful nature may be destroyed and his spirit saved on the day of the Lord' (1 Cor. 5:5).

The churches need to hear about church discipline and get delivered from syrupy sentimentalism! The genuine fear of God is healthy. But I prophesy that 'the church is going into a time in these coming years when we are going to see the judgements of God which are not punishment and they are not discipline, but they are protection to take the person home before they go into further deception.' I believe we are going to see this manifested in the church of God.

The body of Christ needs to get cleaned up of rebels who keep resisting the discipline of God. Some years ago in South Africa there were three men in my congregation who were resisting me, mocking me and undermining my ministry. No one told me about it, but God spoke to my heart and said, 'If they do not repent, they are either going to have to leave the church or otherwise I will take them home.' I turned to my wife and told her what God had told me. I listed the three men's names but I did not tell anyone else.

Within three months two of the men had left the church and the other one was dead.

We have to understand that we are not playing games. God's judgement has already begun in the household of God. He is beginning to clean up the body of Christ.

Free from Guilt

God wants us to be totally free from guilt. He wants us to know that when we fall into sin, the grace of God is there to cleanse us. Jesus is there not to condemn us but to pick us up, if we will be transparent, open and honest about our failings. Remember, we only have the discipline of God to deal with, never his punishment.

Time to reflect:

- Meditate on these words: '[God] is not angry with us, because he has already been angry with us and punished us 2,000 years ago!'
- How has the chapter challenged you in regards to guilt, punishment and God's loving discipline?
- Jesus came and took all the anger and all the wrath and all the punishment of God in our

place. How does this make you want to respond to him? Write a prayer or poem of praise and thanks.

Chapter 6

The Restoration of Dreams

Sometimes the pressure is on us so greatly as Christians, that we want to take off our Christian identity, our uniform, and mingle with the crowd – just be anonymous. We want to say, 'I don't know Jesus, I don't want to live responsibly any more.' I believe that all of us as believers at some time have been in that place. I also believe that God anticipates those times; our Father knows we are going to go through them. He is never disillusioned with us because he never had any illusions in the first place!

His plan is to replace our despair with his wonderful dreams for us. Yes, God gives us grace to fill us with fresh vision and new dreams!

We Need Revelation

Earlier, we considered how much we need a revelation of the character of God. I can't emphasize enough how important this is: one of our greatest needs as believers is to get a *true* and *accurate* revelation of our God – a revelation that he is

- wonderful
- perfect
- pure
- lovely
- awesome
- infinite – he knows the beginning and the end

When he called us he knew the mistakes we were going to make after we got saved. He is never surprised.

God knows that what we are when we are under pressure is what we are in reality. For example, Jesus knew that Peter would deny him. 'I tell you, Peter, before the cock crows today, you will deny three times that you know me' (Lk. 22:34). He also knew that it was Peter who would preach with great boldness on the day of Pentecost. He said to him, 'Simon, Simon, Satan has asked to sift you as wheat. . . . And when you have turned back, strengthen your brothers' (Lk. 22:31,32).

Understand this – failure is OK! Somehow in the mystery of God's economy he expects and allows for our failure. He knows that there is going to be a greater dimension of the grace of God in our lives as a result. There is going to be a greater sense of mercy, compassion and empathy for others.

The Curse of Barrenness

One of the saddest stories to me in the entire Bible is the story of Michal, Saul's daughter. We read about her in 1 and 2 Samuel.

Michal was given to David as a reward for killing Philistines. She was second choice for David after her older sister Merab was given to another. Michal grew up with an insecure father, who once had an anointing, but went into rebellion and became obsessively jealous of David. Saul was a poor example to Michal of what her heavenly Father was like, and she grew up in an environment of impulsiveness, violence and anger.

Unfortunately because of all this, Michal allowed herself to become cynical and sceptical. When David, her husband, brought back the Ark of the Covenant to Jerusalem, he danced with all his might before the Lord, wearing only a loincloth. It was a time of great celebration and praising God. But instead of joining in the radical worship, Michal stood there and laughed at David, criticizing, mocking and ridiculing him in front of everyone. She did not have a good understanding of what God is really like or see him as worthy of extravagant praise. And as a result of her attitude, God pronounced a judgement on Michal that she would be barren for the rest of her life.

I believe that if she had repented, God would have reversed the judgement. If she had softened her heart and turned from criticism and cynicism she could have had the child that she desired. Instead she lived out her life with no fulfilment. She could not conceive and become pregnant, which was a great stigma in her society and time, so there was no positive expectation for her into the future.

Of course, all barrenness is not a result of God's judgement – Michal's was a unique case. There are a number of women mentioned in the Bible who conceived children much later in life and, in every case, their children became champions of faith (Sarah, Leah and Hannah, for example).

Barrenness speaks of loss of hope, loss of vision and loss of aspiration; there is no expectation of ful-filling dreams. How many of you know that if you are just marking time, breathing air, eating food, passing it through your bodies and growing older, you are dead already although you are not in the grave? God wants a people filled with

- hope
- aspirations
- vision
- expectation of fulfilling dreams
- glorious imaginings of things to come

A True Image of God

I believe that until we understand what God is like we are going to be vulnerable to periods in our lives where we are infiltrated with a sceptical, cynical spirit that makes us barren and destroys future hope, aspirations and dreams. I am not only talking about our Christian ministry, but also

- aspirations within our daily work
- aspirations for a better marriage
- aspirations to do well in sport/pastimes
- aspirations to achieve our potential in life
- aspirations for our children
- a future hope

Now, I'm not saying that if we have an aspiration to play for Manchester United or become a movie actor that that dream will necessarily be fulfilled. What I am saying is that we should aspire to reach our potential. In other words, be the best footballer we can be in our local league; be successful in the amateur dramatics society! Whatever our dream, our talents, God has a purpose for them – and a future hope for us.

I have a future hope of seeing churches planted in many nations of the world. I have hope for every area of my life. I dream, I think, I live. Why? Because I am not barren. I understand my Father. If we think God is a hard taskmaster, we will take our talents and bury them for we fear God. If we realize he is not a hard taskmaster, we will take our talents and multiply them because we have vision, a confident hope and expectation for the future.

I refuse to allow people to distort or pervert the image of God to me because the Bible says that 'you will know the truth, and the truth will set you free' (Jn. 8:32). My image of God is formed by Scripture alone. What is God like? He is like Jesus – taking children with runny, snotty noses and dirty feet up onto his lap. Discipline? Yes! Order? Yes! But with humour, fun and laughter, loving them and embracing them. He sees the woman at the well living with a man outside of marriage; she is 'living in sin'. Yet he takes the time to be with her, talk to her, love her and restore her dignity. To the woman caught in the act of adultery, Jesus says, 'Neither do I condemn you . . . Go now and leave your life of sin' (Jn. 8:11). *That* is what God is like. When we read the Bible we see that Jesus is love personified. Jesus came to reveal what God is like . . . God is love.

He is also the God of the second chance, the third chance and the fourth chance. If a righteous man falls seven times, the Lord will lift him up (Prov. 24:16). Why seven times in the book of Proverbs? Once for every day of the week. Every day of the week you can fall and God will lift you up!

Restoration

You know that dream you have held so long in your heart? It isn't destroyed because of your mistake. God is restoring it to you. Let's look at the story of the prodigal (or lost) son (see Lk. 15:11–31). Nowhere in Scripture do we see a clearer picture of God's heart to restore than in this story.

In the beginning, the prodigal is a mess. There in the pigsty he is totally barren. He has lost all vision and aspiration. He has no future dreams of fulfilling his sonship, only servanthood and slavery in his father's house. As he approaches home he rehearses his sad speech. Then, his father runs to meet him and tells his servants to get the 'best robe'.

In the Greek the 'best robe' also means 'first robe'. In Middle Eastern society that indicates position and prestige as being first in line. His father is not saying, 'Let's cover up all that pigsty muck because I am embarrassed by that filth.' He is instead accepting his son into the position of high prestige in his house – first place. This is a picture of what God our Father does for us! When he restores he does a proper job of it. There is no second, third or fourth robe for us. There is a first robe that signifies first-class citizen of the kingdom of God. As soon as we repent and say, 'Lord, I have been wrong,' God forgives us and puts the first robe on us. He also puts a ring on our finger – his stamp of approval.

We are equal heirs with Jesus Christ because of his victory over the devil.

God is an awesome God! He doesn't want our dreams to die because we have sinned and messed up; he wants to restore them. His heart is always to forgive and restore. So don't grieve over the past!

Noah was a righteous man who obeyed God in holy fear, built an ark and preserved human society through a terrible time. Just after that, he was found in a drunken stupor, naked in his tent. He really blew it! So, what does God do about it? He mentions Noah in Hebrews 11 and records Noah among the heroes of the faith!

Abraham's nephew Lot was spared the judgement of Sodom and Gomorrah because of his righteousness. Soon after he escaped the judgement, he was living in a cave and while drunk had incestuous sexual relationships with his daughters. What does God do about that? Centuries later, Peter mentions Lot as a righteous man in one of his New Testament letters (2 Pet. 2:7)!

David was a man who loved God greatly, but also sinned greatly. He committed adultery with Bathsheba, the wife of Uriah the Hittite. When she became pregnant, David recalled Uriah from the battlefield in the hope that he would sleep with his wife. When Uriah wouldn't do so, even after David got him drunk, he was ordered to return to the battlefield. David then gave the command for Uriah to be killed in battle. After Bathsheba had mourned for Uriah, David had her brought to his house. She became his wife and bore him a son.

But the thing David had done displeased the Lord. As a result Nathan the prophet came to David and exposed his sin. He pronounced judgement on David and David quickly repented. David's life was spared but the child became very ill. David pleaded with God for his son; he fasted, went into his house and spent the nights lying on the ground. The elders of his household could not persuade him to get up from the ground or eat food with them. Great depression, discouragement and despair filled David's life at this time.

On the seventh day the child – the son of David and Bathsheba's adulterous union – died. David's response to his son's death startled everyone. He got up from the ground, washed, changed his clothes and went to the house of the Lord to worship. Then he went home to eat.

His servants asked him why he was acting this way. And David replied: 'While the child was still alive, I fasted and wept. I thought, "Who knows? The LORD may be gracious to me and let the child live." But now that he is dead, why should I fast? Can I bring him back again? I will go to him, but he will not return to me' (2 Sam. 12:22,23).

David's focus turned immediately towards the future. He went to Bathsheba, who was now his wife, and lay with her. She conceived again and gave birth to Solomon.

God is so complete in his forgiveness that the child that was born from their married union was the child who became king of Israel and carried the genealogy of Christ. Matthew chapter 1 records the lineage of Christ: Bathsheba, David and Solomon are mentioned in verse 6. The reproductive organs that conceived the child of death, disappointment, disaster and sin were the same organs that conceived a child of destiny, of kings, of royalty and of the lineage of Christ. What was the difference? Repentance!

A Future Hope

David made a deliberate choice not to hold on to the child of the past that represents death and sorrow. He looked to the royal child of the future. He knew there was a future hope and future aspirations waiting to be birthed. He went forward in that hope.

For each one of us, no matter what we have birthed in sin before, or failure before, God has got a Solomon coming. God's delight is to restore our dreams and by his grace to see them fulfilled.

Time to reflect:

- Meditate on these words: 'God is wonderful, perfect, pure, lovely, awesome, infinite – he knows the beginning and the end.'
- When he called us, God knew the mistakes we were going to make. He is never surprised by the things we say or do! How does knowing this add to your security in God?
- God's heart is always to forgive and restore. For that reason, we must not grieve over the past. If

there is anything you need to repent of, do it now, and ask God to restore your dreams – or give you a fresh vision for your life.

Chapter 7

Finding Grace Through the Law

In Chapter 1, I said that grace is the mysterious ability of God to accept us irrespective of our successes or failures. This is because God bases it not on our performance, but on Jesus' performance on our behalf. These are wonderful truths for believers to grasp and live by. However, they should not be thrust at unbelievers until they are ready for them.

God wants us to share our faith and lead others to find the wonderful freedom we have through Christ. The gospel is good news but we must be wise with it. Unbelievers need to be adequately prepared to receive the message of grace. Otherwise we run the risk of offering people 'cheap grace'.

Hell's Best-Kept Secret[2]

Modern evangelism has omitted one key ingredient in leading people to Christ. This missing ingredient in evangelism in the church today is hell's best-kept secret.

Galatians 3:24 and 25 says, 'So the law was put in charge to lead us to Christ that we might be justified by faith. Now that faith has come, we are no longer under the supervision of the law.' We as believers have been justified by faith. But those who do not know Jesus must understand that 'the law was put in charge' to lead them to Christ. Without this understanding they can never come to a true saving faith in Christ. The law in the Bible means the Ten Commandments. This law was given by God to Moses on Mount Sinai.

If the law is not put in charge with the unsaved, there is nothing the Holy Spirit can use to lead them to Christ, for the only thing that will truly lead them to Christ is the Ten Commandments – the law of God! So, the law of God is the essential missing ingredient in evangelism. If unsaved people don't hear the law of God or understand its precepts, they are in danger of coming to Christ without the law and for the wrong reasons. Let me explain – the law itself is powerless to save, but it shows us that we need a Saviour – without this understanding, people might just make an emotional decision not based in seeing their real *need*. So, in truth, only the law can bring them to Christ.

It's true to say, though, that some people accept Christ before they feel the full weight of their sin; also, Jesus reveals himself to those from different religious backgrounds (and none) who have never understood the law. As they grow in their understanding, they then begin to 'see'. But we have to be aware that there are those who are, in effect, false converts who have never come to their Saviour in reality because they have never truly seen their need of salvation. When we make false converts we spend all our time following them up, thinking we're failing because they're backsliding all the time. But they were never properly converted in the first place!

1 Timothy 1:8 says, 'We know that the law is good if one uses it properly.' We do not use the law on the church because the church is released from the law. The purpose of the law is to alert the unsaved to the wrath and judgement of God that is to come.

When I was an unsaved man I was told of the judgement to come. I was judged by the righteous standards of the law and *knew* that I deserved hell. That's how I got converted! Suddenly the message of the cross and grace made sense to me. Through the law I came to Christ and for over twenty years I have lived without backsliding, full of gratitude to him who saved me from the judgement to come . . . whether he gives me a 'good' life or not.

Many Christians view the law as evil and sinful. They know that we're not under law but under grace. But because grace is better, it doesn't mean that the law is evil. The law is good, pure, lovely and beautiful. It reveals the beauty of God's character. David praises God's law in the Psalms. In Psalm

119:77 he says, 'your law is my delight'. In verse 97 he says, 'Oh, how I love your law! I meditate on it all day long.' The words of the law are 'sweeter than honey' to his mouth (v. 103).

The commandments of God are wonderful but they must be used properly. We have to use the law because it brings people to Christ. People who come under the understanding of the law realize that one day they will be judged by the righteous standards of the law. This causes them to flee to the grace of Christ and see that in him they're set free from the law. The law will be written on their hearts and they'll be born again and live for God.

People must come under the law to be set free from it! When they don't understand the law and the judgement to come we can't talk to them about the need to be saved. They'll say, 'Saved? Saved from what?' Once they see that they are going to be judged by the righteous standards of the law, then they want to be saved from judgement. This is the best-kept secret in hell because most of the church does not use the law for conversion. Satan is happy for us to have false converts who constantly have to be propped up and run after.

The law makes people aware

Romans 7:7 says, 'What shall we say, then? Is the law sin? Certainly not! Indeed I would not have known what sin was except through the law.'

The Bible says clearly that without the Ten Commandments nobody will know what sin is. This is how the law leads people to Christ. The law makes people aware of their sin and how they have fallen short of God's standards.

The law leads people to Christ

Many unsaved people would say that they don't believe in the Ten Commandments. They think it is old-fashioned morality that is irrelevant in our sophisticated, modern, secular, humanistic society. It is our job to lovingly help them see that they *do* believe in the Ten Commandments! For instance, if we ask them what they think should happen to someone who is a mass murderer, they would probably say at the very least, 'Lock him up in jail.' We can then say, 'Oh, so you *do* believe in the Ten Commandments! The sixth commandment is "You shall not murder".' Their inner conviction is that murder is wrong and deserves to be punished. Any law, without consequence if you break it, is not a law but just good advice.

The law has to be put in charge again to lead people to Christ. We need to help people understand the Ten Commandments step by step so they can have a genuine conversion. We are not just giving them good advice, but showing them that they are under God's law and there are consequences for breaking this law.

The Ten Commandments

The first commandment is 'You shall have no other gods before me'. Ask the unsaved person you are talking to, 'Have you loved God with all of your heart, soul, mind and strength your whole life, since birth and put him first at all times?' Of course the answer will be 'No.' You can then say to them, 'Well, I'm sorry but you didn't pass that one! God wants nothing to come between him and us.'

Law number two is 'You shall not make for yourself an idol'. God does not want us to make idols with our hands or with our minds. All the graven images that we have made in our minds, all the things we have ever done in secret will be brought out into the open on the Day of Judgement. The basis of determining what comes out in the light is the law of God. That's what we need to impress on people's consciences.

The third commandment is 'You shall not misuse the name of the LORD your God'. Many unsaved people use the name of the Lord as a filthy swear word. Just using it once in this way is enough to break the commandment.

'Remember the Sabbath day by keeping it holy', is the fourth commandment. For twenty-two years of my life I never once took one day a week to rest and reflect on the goodness of God and all that I had. I broke the Sabbath every single week!

Now, the New Testament is very clear in Romans 14 that the church does not have to keep the Jewish

Sabbath. In fact, the early church moved its day of rest from Saturday to Sunday, the first day of the week – the Lord's Day. Let us understand that this day of rest is not a strict religious observance, but it is the provision of God for which we can be grateful – a time to relax and reflect on him, as we recharge our batteries.

'Honour your father and your mother' is the fifth commandment. This means to value them even if they're not the best father and mother. Many people dishonour their father and mother in both word and deed, through hurt, resentment and rebellion.

The sixth commandment is 'You shall not murder'. Most people you witness to will excuse themselves from this one, but Jesus makes it clear in Matthew 5:21 and 22 that anyone who is angry with his brother receives the same judgement as one who murders. There are many babies murdered in the womb through abortion. It's not just the girls and women involved who are responsible, but also the parents and partners who contribute to the decisions.

'You shall not commit adultery' is the seventh commandment. We must understand that sex outside of marriage in any form with any partner is not right. The Bible very clearly says that the only place for sex is within marriage between a man and a woman. Sex outside of marriage is breaking the commandment. Many people fall short on this one and try to justify it, but you can't select which commandments you believe in. If mass murderers deserve punishment for killing people and breaking the commandments, so do adulterers. In Matthew 5:28 Jesus says, 'But I tell you that anyone who looks at a woman lustfully has already committed adultery with her in his heart.' Jesus is saying here that *just looking* makes a person guilty.

'You shall not steal' is the eighth commandment. What makes a person a thief? Is it the value of the thing that you steal or the act of stealing itself? You are a thief because you steal, whether you steal a million pounds or 50p from the tax office.

The ninth commandment is 'You shall not give false testimony against your neighbour'. This means that you can tell no lies, exaggerations or fibs. There's no such thing as 'a little white lie' because there's not white murder, white adultery or white stealing. Everyone will admit to telling lies at some time or other.

'You shall not covet' is the tenth and final commandment. The Bible elaborates on how this refers to coveting any of another person's possessions and includes jealousy, envy, lust, greed and materialism.

After we have gone through the Ten Commandments with the unsaved person, we then need to help them see how they personally fall short. James 2:10 says, 'For whoever keeps the whole law and yet stumbles at just one point is guilty of breaking all of it.' We need to say to the unsaved person, 'Now, that is the way God's going to judge you on the Day of Judgement! If you just break one law, just one, you're guilty and will be judged.'

We must remember not to preach grace and the cross to people until they are ready for it, because otherwise it is, in effect, like casting pearls before swine! We must let people feel the true weight of their sin. They must be conscious of the fact that they are wrong before they can see that their only hope is what Jesus did on the cross for them. We must try not to appeal to their emotions but convert them through the law; often people are begging for a way out when they have truly faced their sin!

The truth is, you have to know you are a sinner before you value the cross. Amazingly some people – after they have heard the law – say, 'Well, I don't know if I really need to be forgiven.' Perhaps we can help them with an anecdote like this.

Once there was a little girl who watched the sheep grazing in a pasture of green grass. The sheep looked so white to her against the background of green grass. Then it began to snow. As the snow came down the whole backdrop turned white. The sheep began to look a little dirty against the white background. Same sheep – different background . . . so, different perspective!

When we compare ourselves to the background of human standards, we look reasonably clean. For example, when we compare ourselves to our friends who drink, swear and cheat more than us,

we look quite good. And when we compare ourselves to someone like Adolf Hitler, we look *very*
good! However, God is not going to judge us by the
standards of humanity, but by the snowy white
righteousness of his law.

When we have the snowy white background of
the law of God, we see we are not as clean as we
thought. It's at this point that people admit, 'Oh,
I've made a mistake. I've been measuring myself by
human standards and not by the standards of God's
law.' This is the time to start sharing the good news!

Through the Law to Grace

When someone has been led to Jesus through the
law, grace suddenly has major significance in their
lives. After examining themselves in the light of
each of the Ten Commandments, and realizing that
breaking only one of them makes them a prime can-
didate for judgement and punishment, grace seems
very appealing! The grace of God takes on major
importance because they have felt the weight of the
law. Grace releases them from the burden of having
to keep the law.

But we need to have the wisdom of God to know
when to use the law and when not to.

When Paul was preaching to the Jews who knew
all about the law of God, he mostly preached grace
and the cross, seldom the law. But when he went to

the Gentiles in Athens, he preached the law and called for repentance.

If an unsaved person is from, say, a Roman Catholic background they will know all about the Ten Commandments. We must preach Jesus, the cross and grace to them. If someone doesn't know the law, we must lovingly share it with them. Although we need to show them serious issues – how they've sinned, where they've sinned and how seriously God will judge them (for the purpose of the law is essentially to undermine confidence in our own self-righteousness) – we do need to do this with a twinkle in our eye, with a gentle voice and most importantly of all, with *love*. And we must remember, especially when we are dealing with people who are outcasts in society, like prostitutes or homosexuals, some people need first to *experience* grace before they can face the law. So we need to love them, show interest in them, let them see we're normal, sane, friendly and caring. In short, we need to earn the right to speak to them. And if people are not ready to hear about the law and be led into grace, we must not push them. We must exercise grace as we try to lead people into grace!

When they are ready, people who come to Jesus through the law are thoroughly converted. Grace explodes into their lives with joy and freedom. They realize that grace is not about what we do for God, but what God does for us!

Time to reflect:

- Meditate on these words: 'Grace is not about what we do for God, but what God does for us!'
- How has this chapter challenged you in regards to sharing the gospel with outcasts, and with people who would say they don't believe in the Ten Commandments?
- Perhaps you know someone who has had a 'false conversion'. Pray for them and ask God to give them a sense of their very real need of grace.

Chapter 8

Grace Unlimited

God has grace in abundance, totally unlimited, waiting for us to tap into. John 1:16 says, 'From the fulness of his grace we have all received one blessing after another.'

God pours out one blessing after another and before one blessing has finished the next one is already on its way. His will for us is to receive blessing upon blessing, going from one degree of glory to the next degree of glory.

Grace Multiplied

How can we understand the extent of God's grace? With our finite minds we can never fully understand the length, breadth, height and depth of God's grace.

When we get a revelation of how good God is and how much he wants to bless us, we can break free from old cynical mindsets. If we can catch just a glimpse of the goodness of God, of what he is really like, we are overcome by his awesome splendour. If we take that and multiply it by a trillion billion times we might just be scratching below the surface of what God is really like in all of his goodness!

Breaking Mindsets

Cynicism and scepticism are curses on our lives. We say things like, 'That's too good to be true.' Where and how did we reach that conclusion? What logical premise did we start with to assume such a stupid thing: that something is too good to be true? Who made us think that things are only true if they're bad? Who's been playing with our brains?

Breaking Down the Barriers

We need to keep getting set free from images in our minds that are negative about God. We read in 2 Peter 3:18: 'But grow in the grace and knowledge of our Lord and Saviour Jesus Christ.'

Knowledge of God means experiencing God and knowing him better and better. When this happens more and more grace flows in our lives.

We have to protect our knowledge of God. Satan tries his hardest to keep us from grace and constantly

tries to deceive us. How do we protect our knowledge of God?

> We demolish arguments and every pretension that
> sets itself up against the knowledge of God, and we
> take captive every thought to make it obedient to
> Christ. (2 Cor. 10:5)

God wants every barrier between us and him to be
broken down.

God Hates Separation!

Isaiah 43:25 says, 'I, even I, am he who blots out
your transgressions, for my own sake, and remembers your sins no more.' Isn't it amazing that God
blots out our transgressions and he totally forgets
the sins we've done – for his sake? We would think
it was for our sake, but he says it's for his sake! I
believe the reason the Lord says this is because he
loves us so much. He loves to be with us and
enjoys being close to us. He wants to hug us and
kiss us and make us a success. When we sin he
can't do that because our sin stands between us
and him. He hates it when we sin because sin
causes separation and then he misses us. He blots
out our sin for his own sake, so he can put his arms
around us again and welcome us back into intimacy.

Grace Brings Power

When we as individuals begin to grasp how good God is, then we corporately, as the church of Jesus Christ, will rise more and more in glory.

As we understand the heart of God towards us, his wonderful unmerited favour, his boundless grace, his desire to shower blessing after blessing upon us, we begin to change our expectation of life and the future and to move in power.

Acts 4:33 talks of the New Testament church and how '. . . much grace was upon them all'. Verse 34 says, 'There were no needy persons among them.' When grace comes on a church, all needs are met. That includes physical and financial needs, relational needs and spiritual needs.

Grace and Revelation

God always intended that the church of Jesus Christ would be built upon the revelation of who he is.

Jesus asked his disciples, 'Who do you say I am?' (Mt. 16:15). Peter put aside any negative thoughts, doubts or fears and boldly proclaimed, 'You are the Christ, the Son of the living God' (v. 16). Jesus knew that Peter was having spirit to spirit communication with his Father. He said, 'Blessed are you,

Simon son of Jonah, for this was not revealed to
you by man, but by my Father in heaven. And I tell
you that you are Peter, and on this rock I will build
my church, and the gates of Hades will not overcome it' (vv. 17,18). Jesus was saying here that he
would build his church on the revelation of who he
was.

Revelation Unlocks an Abundance of Grace

Peter had a further revelation of who Jesus was when
Jesus said to him, 'Do you love me? . . . Feed my
sheep' (see Jn. 21:17). Grace was multiplied in his life
and shortly afterwards he got up and preached and
3,000 people were saved in one day.

Grace got behind Peter in the form of a mighty
rushing wind and blew him into the next phase
of God's purpose for his life. He could then
write, 'Grace and peace be yours in abundance
through the knowledge of God and of Jesus our
Lord' (2 Pet. 1:2). Grace increased in his life so
that even his shadow was enough to heal the sick
(see Acts 5:15)! God multiplied his goodness to
him.

One day he fell into a trance and had another revelation from God (see Acts 10). He was radically
catapulted in a new direction and a door to the
Gentile world opened. God increased the anointing
on his life.

The Anointing Brings Grace

We talked earlier about the channels of grace. But the essential ingredient God gives to bring grace into our lives is the anointing – the tangible substance and essence of God's presence. The anointing comes into every single area of our lives. Isaiah 61:1–7 speaks of the anointing that came upon Jesus and is there for us as well. It is so that we can preach good news to the poor, bind up the brokenhearted, proclaim freedom for the captives, release from darkness for the prisoners and proclaim the year of the Lord's favour. The greater the anointing upon a person's life, the greater the measure of grace.

Grace in Reconciliation

God's great love for us is wonderfully demonstrated in Romans 5:8: 'While we were still sinners, Christ died for us.' God didn't wait for us to become nice clean Christians before he loved us. He didn't wait for us to repent. The Bible says that while we were his enemies he was so in love with us that 'we were reconciled to him through the death of his Son' (Rom. 5:10).

To reconcile means to make right with. While we were living in sin God made us right with himself. This is amazing. If God loved us that much while we were enemies, how much more does he love us as Christians, even when we mess up, sin and fail? '. . . how much more, having been reconciled, shall we be saved through his life!' (Rom. 5:10).

Romans 5:7 tells us, 'Very rarely will anyone die for a righteous man, though for a good man someone might possibly dare to die' (Rom. 5:7). But while we were still in our sin, Jesus died for us. This is definitely not acting according to human wisdom! But it must make us stop and think. How should we be treating those who are 'still sinners'?

Sinners are people who are outside of God's kingdom. They can be doctors, lawyers, teachers, refuse collectors, members of parliament, prostitutes or factory workers. They can be homosexual, heterosexual, bisexual. There are no categories of sinners. A sinner can be a militant person who believes it is right to use violence and terror. But a sinner can also be a 'decent' person who is happily married, goes to work eight hours a day, never drinks and gives to charity. The fact is, that person is still lost and is an enemy of God until they discover his love, repent of their sin and enter into a relationship with him.

God wants us to love all sinners like he does. So, when we walk into a pub and see someone drunk, our attitude should be the same as God's. We should not wait for this person to repent, get baptized and cleaned up before we show them reconciliation. God has already reconciled this person (while they were still a sinner) and therefore we should treat them the way we would treat the most holy Christian. We have to remember that Jesus has already paid the price for their reconciliation.

In 2 Corinthians 5:18, we read that Christ has given us 'the ministry of reconciliation'. He has 'committed to us the message of reconciliation' (v.19) and 'We are therefore Christ's ambassadors, as though God were making his appeal through us' (v. 20). *This* then should be our attitude towards those who are not saved – God is making his appeal through us. If we have a spirit of reconciliation we have favour in our hearts towards people who don't know God.

Sometimes we see people doing wrong and we just want to straighten them out. But God can't let us loose when we have attitudes of unrighteous rejection. Jesus was called the friend of sinners because that is what he was in reality. He loved people. He didn't befriend people just to target them for conversion! He lifted people up and restored their dignity. He cared about them – who they were and how they felt. We need to follow his example and treat sinners as though they were already saved. These people need to see our love, gentleness, humility, boldness, compassion, reality, honesty, integrity and reconciling spirit. This is grace in action.

Focusing on Jesus

I believe we need to focus again on Jesus as the reference point for unsaved people. We are not called to reconcile people to us but to reconcile them to him. We are not called to reconcile people to our way of thinking, our behaviour or our religious culture. It is to Jesus and Jesus alone that we must point them otherwise we cramp people and stereotype them, putting them into so-called 'Christian' boxes. It's Jesus they need to meet. He will lead them into abundant life that is full and free and invigorating. He will lead them into all truth.

God is Heaps Better than We Think!

As God pours out grace unlimited upon us, we understand more and more who he really is. God is multifaceted and multi-talented, but I am not talking now about his attributes. I'm talking about who he is, his essence, his substance and his intrinsic being. The Bible says he is three things. In 1 John 4:16 we read 'God is love', 1 John 1:5 says 'God is light' and John 4:24 says 'God is spirit'. God is love, God is light, God is spirit. What does that mean?

God is love

To say that God is love does not mean that God has love. It means that his whole being, everything that he is, is eternally disposed to show unfailing pure love towards us.

There is nothing we can do to stop God loving us. For God to stop loving us he would have to stop being who he is, because he is love. We need to remember this at those times when we think God has stopped loving us because we've blown it and messed up. For God to stop loving us is for God to stop being who he is!

God is light

The Bible says that God is light. This refers to his majesty, his magnificence, his glory, his power and his truth. All of God is light, but throughout Scripture that primarily refers to God's moral character. God is light. God is a moral being. He doesn't have morals and good manners. God is morality, God is good manners. He will never do anything immoral to us. He'll never manipulate us, he'll never abuse us, he'll never send us anywhere that he didn't call, anoint and enable us to go. He'll never require anything of us that we can't do, because God is light. He's pure integrity, loveliness, beauty and morality. How can we fellowship with such a being? Because of Jesus. God remembers our sin no more because he's so madly in love with us.

God is spirit

God is spirit . . . What does that actually mean? It means that we will never be able to contact or understand God with our flesh or with our brains. As clever as we might think we are, we could never keep up with God!

God has infinite unlimited intelligence. His dimension is beyond the comprehension of human IQ. Does that mean he is irrational and illogical? No. God created reason, logic and rationale. But he operates above these human levels. He is 'super-rational'. Reason has to rest in revelation.

We are created in the image of God, and if God is essentially a spirit being, then on the inside of our bodies we are a spirit. With our soul, mind and emotions we contact the intellectual, emotional world. With our physical bodies we touch, taste, see, smell and hear the physical world. With our spirit we contact God. Our spirit has the capacity to comprehend God, not in the language of our brain, but in spirit language. With him we have spirit to spirit communication.

So, our spirit has the supernatural capacity to fellowship with God, contact God, comprehend God, commune with God and touch God!

God Gives Grace to the Humble

We cannot understand the full implications of what it means that God is love, God is light and God is spirit. We have to be humble and acknowledge that God is super-intelligent and knows far more than any of us.

In 1 Peter 5:5 we read, 'God opposes the proud but gives grace to the humble.' Humble people are not those who 'put themselves down'. Truly humble people are those who acknowledge their total dependence on God. It is only our pride that keeps us from grace – the more we depend on God, the more grace we receive from him. We can never depend on God too much. His supply of grace is totally unlimited.

God is heaps better than we think!

Time to reflect:

- Meditate on these words: 'God remembers our sin no more because he's so madly in love with us.'
- We have read that as we understand the heart of God towards us, his wonderful unmerited favour and boundless grace, his desire to shower blessings upon us, we begin to change our expectation of life and the future and to move in power. How has your expectation for your own life and future changed since you picked up this book?
- Ask God to pour out his grace upon you today. Ask him for his wonderful anointing so you might know his presence and power. How might you share what you have learned in *Living in the Grace of God* with others who don't yet know him?

Endnotes

[1] A.W. Tozer, *The Root of the Righteous* (Harrisburg, PA: Christian Publications, Inc.).

[2] Some of the insight for this chapter and the phrase 'Hell's best-kept secret' came from a small book called *Hell's Best Kept Secret* by Ray Comfort (Living Waters Publications).